MW01110206

Seeds of a Nation

OKLAHOMA

Oklahoma

Deanne Durrett

KIDHAVEN
PRESS™

THOMSON

GALE

San Diego • Detroit • New York • San Francisco • Cleveland
New Haven, Conn. • Waterville, Maine • London • Munich

THOMSON

GALE

™

On cover: Settlers set up a tent city after a land run.

For more information, contact
KidHaven Press
27500 Drake Rd.
Farmington Hills, MI 48331-3535
Or you can visit our Internet site at http://www.gale.com

LIBRARY OF CONGRESS CATALOGING-IN-PUBLICATION DATA

Durrett, Deanne, 1940–
  Oklahoma / by Deanne Durrett.
    p. cm.—(Seeds of a nation)
Summary: Traces the history of Oklahoma, focusing on the ancient Clovis culture, nomadic Wichita tribes, European exploration, the creation of Indian Territory, white settlement during the Boomer Movement, and statehood in 1907.
Includes bibliographical references and index.
  ISBN 0-7377-1479-4 (alk. paper)
  1. Oklahoma—History—Juvenile literature. 2. Oklahoma—Juvenile literature. [1. Oklahoma—History.] I. Title. II. Series.
  F694.3 .D87 2003
  976.6—dc21

                                                                    2002152144

Printed in the United States of America

Contents

Chapter One

A Long History of Settlement

Oklahoma, the forty-sixth state, is located in the heart of North America. Texas borders the state on the south and west. New Mexico touches the western end of the panhandle. Colorado, Kansas, Missouri, and Arkansas form the north and east borders.

Long ago a land of rolling prairies, mountains, lakes, running creeks, and rivers lay in the heartland of North America. The first people who lived here did not have a written language. As a result, they did not leave a written record of their history. No one knows who they were or what they called themselves. As they lived their daily lives, however, they left clues about themselves.

Over thousands of years, erosion and buildup buried the clues. From time to time, however, these clues rise to the surface for archaeologists to discover. When the first few spearheads, pottery shards, and ancient bones were found, archaeologists searched for more. Archaeologists study these **artifacts** so they can know about life in the time before recorded history.

Prehistoric hunters spear a mammoth trapped in mud.

Alaska

New Hampshire

Minnesota
Washington
Wisconsin
Michigan
Vermont
Main
Oregon
Montana
North
Dakota
Great Lakes
New York
Massac.
Idaho
South
Dakota
Indiana
Rh
Isla
Wyoming
Nebraska
Iowa
Ohio
Conr
New Jer
Nevada
Illinois
Pennsylva
Utah
Colorado
Delaware
California
Kansas
Missouri
Kentucky
Maryland
Arizona
New
Mexico
Oklahoma
Tennessee
Virginia
West Virginia
Georgia
North Carolina
Texas
South Carolina
Hawaii
Louisiana
Alabama
Florida
Arkansas
Mississippi

Oklahoma's Place in the United States Today

The Clovis Culture

In 1961 archaeologists found the bones of a mammoth
and the hunters' spearheads that killed it near Anadarko,
Oklahoma. The mammoth died about eleven thousand
years ago. Spearheads they had found at other sites helped
them identify the hunters. These early craftsmen made
flint spearheads by chipping the stone away to form the
desired shape. Two types of ancient spearheads have been
found. Scientists have identified the people who made
these spearheads as the Clovis and Folsom cultures. (Clovis spearheads were first found near Clovis, New Mexico.
The Folsom spearheads were first found near Folsom,
New Mexico.) The spearheads found near Anadarko
matched the spearheads found near Clovis, New Mexico.

This meant that the hunters who killed this mammoth in Oklahoma belonged to the Clovis culture.

The people of the Clovis culture are the oldest known inhabitants of North America. They were hunter-gatherers who followed the mammoth and bison that roamed the central areas of the continent. They ate the meat of the animals they killed and gathered wild plants for food and medicine. They were nomads, which means they did not build permanent homes or villages. As a result, the only evidence of their existence is stone spearheads, knife blades, and a few tools made from mammoth bones. The Clovis culture disappeared from North America between eight

Spearheads made by the Folsom have finely sharpened points.

and nine thousand years ago. From the clues they left, we know that the Folsom culture replaced the Clovis culture and that the Folsom had improved spearhead-making skills.

More Recent Cultures

Archaeologists have also found evidence of more recent farming and hunting cultures in Oklahoma. These people lived in the Oklahoma area from the tenth to fifteenth centuries A.D. (six to eleven hundred years ago). They located their villages along the Wichita and Canadian Rivers and the creeks that flowed into these rivers. They grew corn, beans, and squash in the fertile soil of the floodplains. They also hunted bison and deer and fished. Four different cultures are known to have lived in the area that is now western and southern Oklahoma during that time. They had no written language and left no written history. No one knows what these people called themselves. When Spanish explorers reached Oklahoma in the sixteenth century, they found people who called themselves the Teyas and the Escanjaques. Archaeologists believe that these tribes descended from the four earlier cultures. The modern-day Wichita Indians descended from the Teyas and Escanjaques.

Wichita Indians

Because the Wichita descended from the Teyas and Escanjaques, they are indigenous (native) to the region.

The Wichita built permanent villages along the Arkansas River and farmed the fertile delta. This area is

A Native American on horseback hunts a bison with bow and arrow.

in present-day Kansas. Their round grass one-room houses had a smoke hole in the center of the roof. The women in the household cooked on a fire beneath the smoke hole and ground grain for bread nearby. When night came, the whole family slept in that one room. Some houses were large enough for twenty beds.

From planting season to harvest, the Wichita lived in their permanent villages. From fall to spring, the Wichita became nomadic hunters. Their hunting grounds extended into Oklahoma beyond the Canadian River. During this time they followed the herd and lived in **tepees**. They camped on the prairie while the herd grazed nearby. When the buffalo moved on, the Wichita broke camp and followed.

The Wichita Nation was divided into several **bands**. Each band followed its own leader. These individual bands were united into one nation by culture, tradition, religion, and lifestyle. Members of each band traveled and camped together during hunting season. They clustered their permanent circular grass-thatched houses in villages along waterways. Spanish explorer Francisco Vásquez de Coronado was the first European to visit the Wichita. He estimated that twenty-five villages stretched along the Arkansas River, which extends from Kansas into Oklahoma.

The Wichita lived in round houses, similar to this one, made of grass.

Spanish explorers forcefully relocate Native Americans, using spears to prod them along.

These early inhabitants of Oklahoma roamed the land freely and in peace. The scene changed, however, when European settlement forced the relocation of other tribes in the area.

The Osage moved into the northeastern area of Oklahoma about 1796. By 1800 the Comanche had control of land that is now western Oklahoma, the Texas panhandle, and part of New Mexico. They called their land the Comancheria. The Kiowa settled in land west of the Comancheria. These tribes were hunters and raiders and one tribe often warred against another. As a result, when American explorers arrived in Oklahoma, long after the Spanish and French, they faced hostile Indians as well as a vast and rugged land.

Chapter Two

In Search of
the Lost City
of Gold

The first explorers came to Oklahoma in search of gold. They were driven by greed and an old Spanish **legend** based on a historical event. According to history, African Muslims (called Moors) invaded Spain in 711. The Moors occupied Spain until 1492. According to the legend, during the time the Moors occupied Spain, seven **bishops** and their followers escaped. They sailed west to the New World and found riches. The settlements they established were said to be made of gold.

Many years later, Spain established colonies in Mexico. In 1539 Fray Marcos de Niza, a Franciscan living in Mexico City, made the first expedition into the Southwest in search of the Seven Cities of Gold. He claimed to have seen one of them, Cibola. He described Cibola as bigger than Mexico City. The Indians told him that Cibola was the smallest of the Seven Cities of Gold. The legend and this eyewitness account **enticed** Spanish explorers into the heartland of North America. Although they found Indian villages that gleamed in the sun from a distance, they never found gold.

The legend of Cibola, a city made of gold, lured Spanish explorers to Oklahoma.

Coronado

Francisco Vásquez de Coronado was the first European to reach the land that would become Oklahoma. He came from a Spanish colony in Mexico but had no plan to establish more colonies or map the new world.

He invested a large amount of his own money and borrowed from his wealthy wife to buy food and supplies for his expedition. He also hired an army of almost three hundred men to help him conquer what he believed to be the Seven Cities of Gold.

Coronado set out from Mexico in 1540. He traveled north into what is now Arizona, east into New Mexico and west Texas, then north across the Oklahoma panhandle into Kansas. He did not make friends with the Indians. He traveled with a large army and each tribe he met wanted him to move on. To get him to leave, each tribe assured him that the Cities of Gold existed and gave him directions leading him out of their territory. After reaching the Wichita villages in Kansas, Coronado gave up and began the long journey back to Mexico.

Other Spanish explorers also came into the heartland of North America in search of the legendary gold. None of them found it. Still, Spain claimed the region and blocked French exploration until the 1700s.

Fur Traders

French explorers sought wealth from another source—**pelts**. Fur-bearing animals including beaver, otter, mink, and muskrat were common in the area. The furs from these animals could be sold in Europe for gold. The

Francisco Vásquez de Coronado (background) led an army across the Oklahoma panhandle in search of gold.

Indians were expert tanners. In addition to these furs, beautifully tanned buffalo robes were available in every Indian village.

French fur traders traded metal tools and other items for the furs. These included knives, axes, hatchets, hoes, kettles, and needles, plus brightly colored cloth, beads, and mirrors. The traders sold the furs in Europe at a huge profit while the Indians treasured the items from France that made their life easier.

The French traders established trading posts where Indians could come to trade. The French wanted to expand this profitable business by establishing more trading posts. As a result, they did some exploring on their own and eagerly followed the routes of others.

French Explorers

Bernard de La Harpe led the first French expedition into the Oklahoma area in 1719. He explored the southeastern part along the Red River to the mouth of the Kiamitia. He returned to the region in 1721. This time, he explored the eastern section along the Arkansas River. French fur traders followed de La Harpe and other explorers into the area, which later became part of the Louisiana Purchase.

Louisiana Purchase

At the close of the French and Indian War in 1763, French possessions west of the Mississippi were given to Spain. This area was called the Province of Louisiana. Forty years later, Spain returned the Province of

An Indian woman tans a buffalo skin to trade for European products.

French fur traders conduct business with the Wichita.

Louisiana to France. Throughout this time, although the land belonged to Spain, French traders continued business as usual. About the time the land returned to France, the Chouteau brothers, French fur traders, established the first permanent white settlement in Oklahoma. This trading post became present-day Salina, Oklahoma.

Almost immediately after regaining the land, France sold the vast region to the United States in 1803 for $15 million. The Louisiana Purchase almost doubled the size of the United States. Thirteen states in the Midwest, including Oklahoma, would eventually be carved from the Louisiana Purchase.

American Explorers

The Louisiana Purchase became final in May 1804. Almost immediately, the U.S. government sent expeditions to explore the new possession. Lewis and Clark led the most famous American expedition. They left St. Louis in 1804 to travel up the Missouri River to the Rocky Mountains and on through Oregon to the Pacific Coast.

In July 1820, U.S. Army major Stephen H. Long began an expedition in the Rocky Mountains to follow

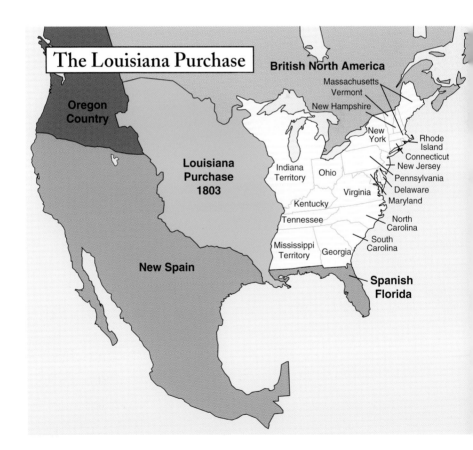

The Louisiana Purchase

British North America

Massachusetts
Vermont
New Hampshire

Oregon Country

New York
Rhode Island
Connecticut
New Jersey

Louisiana Purchase 1803

Indiana Territory
Ohio

Pennsylvania
Delaware
Maryland

Virginia

Kentucky

Tennessee

North Carolina

South Carolina

Mississippi Territory
Georgia

New Spain

Spanish Florida

the Red River south and east. Near the completion of the expedition in 1821, he discovered that he had traveled the Canadian River. As a result, he explored the central area of what is now Oklahoma from west to east. From the Rockies, across west Texas, and into the Oklahoma region he found a flatland he called "The Great American Desert." Long and the other explorers who visited the area reported that the treeless plain was worthless and unfit for habitation by anyone except Indians. As a result, the whole Louisiana Purchase became **Indian Country**—for a while.

Chapter Three

Indian Territory

In 1803, the year of the Louisiana Purchase, Ohio became the seventeenth state. As the United States grew, settlement moved west. Indian tribes in the northeast gradually moved west. They crowded the tribes living in the upper Mississippi and Ohio valleys. Those tribes moved west and south across the Mississippi River.

Dwindling Land

To create an official place for these tribes, Congress created **Indian Territory** in 1834. This territory included all the land west of the Mississippi except Arkansas Territory and the states of Louisiana and Missouri. As other territories west of the Mississippi became states, tribes that were displaced by white settlement gradually moved from the northern plains to the southern plains. By 1854, Indian Territory had shrunk to a strip of land as wide as

Indian tribes were driven from their native lands by white settlement.

present-day Oklahoma (without the panhandle), stretching from South Dakota to Texas. When Kansas and Nebraska became states, Indian Territory dwindled to the area that is now Oklahoma (without the panhandle).

As white settlement demanded more land, Congress passed laws to relocate tribes to Indian Territory. This action was called **removal**. The tribes actually ceded (gave up) their vast lands in the east for a smaller homeland in Indian Territory. During this time, the Indian population decreased greatly. Many were killed in battle. And large numbers died of disease or starvation. Many more died during removal.

The Five Civilized Tribes

The Five Civilized Tribes, so called because they had adopted many customs of the whites, were the first tribes to be removed to the part of Indian Territory that is now Oklahoma. These tribes, the Cherokee, Choctaw, Chickasaw, Creek, and Seminole, lived in the area that is now Tennessee, Virginia, North and South Carolina, Georgia, Alabama, Mississippi, Louisiana, Arkansas, and Florida.

The Choctaw moved to the Oklahoma area in 1820 while the other four tribes delayed removal as long as they could. The Cherokee fought removal in court and won. The U.S. government responded by passing new and stronger laws forcing removal. And the Seminole went to war against the United States. No treaty was signed to end the war. However, the fighting ended and most Seminole were relocated by 1842.

Once settled in the Oklahoma region, the Five Civilized Tribes worked to rebuild their societies. Before long each tribe had formed a constitutional government, with a powerful judicial system and a strong economy. They also established schools for their children.

Billy Bowlegs, a Seminole chief, led his people to war with the United States.

The Plains Tribes

At this time, most of what is now Oklahoma (except the panhandle and an area of unassigned land in the heart of the state) was officially given to the Five Civilized Tribes as their homeland. Little attention was given to the tribes that already claimed hunting ground there, including the Comanche and Kiowa. These tribes began raiding the tribes that had invaded their land.

As more states joined the Union, the Five Civilized Tribes were forced to cede their western lands in Indian Territory to make room to relocate tribes from the Northern Plains. The Comanche and Kiowa had already claimed some of this land as part of their hunting ground. As the relocated tribes **encroached** on their hunting territory, the Kiowa and Comanche grew more hostile and increased their raids.

The U.S. Army was called in to put an end to the hostilities. In 1864 Colonel Christopher Carson (Kit Carson) led a regiment of U.S. troops into the Comancheria. This was the beginning of a ten-year battle to defeat the last free-roaming Indians. These included the Apache, Kiowa, and Comanche. The survivors would be relocated to a reservation in the southwestern part of Indian Territory near present-day Lawton, Oklahoma. The struggle ended when Comanche chief Quanah Parker, the last war chief of the Comanches, surrendered in June 1875. Parker believed that surrender to life on the reservation was the only way to save his people. As he led the last band of Comanches through

A Comanche warrior. Relocation of Indians forced his tribe from their home in the Northern Plains.

the gates at Fort Sill, Oklahoma, he planned to help his people accept life on the reservation.

According to treaties between the federal government and Indian tribes, Indian Territory belonged to the Indians that were relocated there. To uphold these treaties, federal law did not allow white settlement in Indian Territory. The U.S. Army enforced this law. This would change, however, as the demand for land increased and the Oklahoma area was viewed through the eyes of settlers heading west. To meet this demand for land the U.S. government would break its promise to the Indians again.

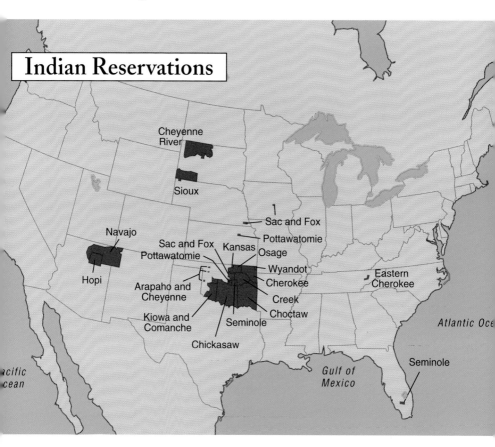

Indian Reservations

Oklahoma Trails

When gold was discovered in California, Indian Territory lay in the pathway to the west. The California Road linked Fort Smith, Arkansas, to Santa Fe, New Mexico. It followed the Canadian River across Indian Territory and through the Comancheria, connecting with other routes to California at Santa Fe. Wagon trains following this route brought an almost constant flow of people across Indian Territory from east to west.

A wagon train bound for California makes its way across Indian Territory.

In addition, Texas cattle ranchers drove their herds across Indian Territory on their way to the railroads in Kansas. These cattle drives passed through Indian Territory along the Shawnee Trail, the Chisholm Trail, and the Great Western Trail. The cattle drives crossed Indian Territory from south to north.

People who traveled these trails discovered that the explorers had been wrong. This land was not a Great American Desert. It was a land they wanted to settle. It soon came to their attention that about 2 million acres in the heart of Indian Territory had not been assigned to any tribe. Some people urged Congress to open these lands to white settlement. This was called the Boomer Movement and it brought about the creation of Oklahoma Territory.

Chapter Four

Boomers and Sooners

In 1879 the *Chicago Times* published an article calling attention to the unassigned land in Indian Territory. Other newspapers soon joined in promoting the idea of white settlement in these lands. Some people, members of the Boomer Movement, wanted to change the federal law to allow white settlement in Indian Territory.

Boomer Movement

David Louis Payne was the first leader of the Boomer Movement. He made speeches and lobbied Congress to open this section of Indian Territory to white settlement. In violation of the law, he also led wagon trains into Indian Territory trying to establish colonies in the unassigned lands. These settlers were turned back and escorted across the Kansas line. Some entered the forbidden land again and again. They wanted to be arrested for trying to settle in the unassigned lands so the law could be tested in court.

In 1887, the Boomer Movement gained strength with completion of the Santa Fe Railroad through the heart of the unassigned lands. In February 1889, Congress finally passed a bill that allowed settlement of the unassigned lands. President Grover Cleveland signed the bill into law on March 2, 1889. On March 23, Benjamin

Standing on a horse, a Wichita tries to turn back settlers at the border of Indian Territory.

Harrison (the new president) set the date and time for opening the unassigned lands to settlement—at noon on April 22, 1889.

The 1889 Land Run

Land was available on a first-come basis. People who wanted land lined up along the border of the unassigned lands. When the cannon sounded at noon, they raced into the unassigned lands and staked a claim for the land they wanted to settle. Those who waited for the boom of the cannon at noon were called Boomers. Some, however, did not wait until noon. They slipped across the line the night before. These early arrivals were called Sooners. For this reason, Oklahoma is called the Sooner State.

Settlers rush to claim land in Oklahoma during the 1889 land run.

Between fifty and seventy-five thousand people participated in this first land run. About one-third of them acquired land. Some staked a claim for 160 acres of farm land. Others claimed a city lot to build a business or a home in a new city. The land was free to any adult American citizen who was head of a family. Official filing of the claim required a fourteen-dollar filing fee. Within the next six months, the homesteader had to build on the property and begin living there.

Cities sprang up instantly that April day. By sundown, Guthrie and Oklahoma Station (present-day Oklahoma City) swelled from a population of a few railroad workers, government officials, soldiers, and deputy marshals to tent cities of more than ten thousand people.

About the same time that Congress moved toward opening the unassigned lands, they passed another bill that would eventually open the rest of Oklahoma for settlement—the Dawes Act.

The Dawes Act

The tribes owned reservation lands as a community. As a result, no individual Indian owned land and no Indian land could be sold. Thus, there could be no white settlement. The government wanted to change this. Senator Henry Dawes thought that if Indians each owned land individually, they would be more likely to become more "American" and less "Indian." At the time, most Americans wanted the Indians to adopt white ways. Whites also saw it as a way of opening land that was unoccupied to white settlement. Dawes introduced a bill to make it

Homesteaders migrate to Oklahoma to begin living on the land they claimed.

possible to divide Indian lands into individual parcels. Each qualified tribal member would receive an **allotment** of land. The bill passed in 1887.

One by one, tribal lands were opened for settlement under the Dawes Act. After the Indians received their allotments, the remaining land was opened for white settlement. Four more land runs brought white settlers to Oklahoma. The last land run opened the Cherokee Outlet (Cherokee hunting grounds, not their homelands) in 1893. In the next few years, the other tribal lands were opened for settlement until all the reservations were gone.

The Dawes Act, however, did not apply to the Cherokee, Chickasaw, Choctaw, Creek, and Seminole who had been relocated and given land by treaties. The lands of these Indian nations were not reservations. Soon after the act was passed, Indian agents (government employees sent to help manage Indian affairs) pressured these tribal leaders into agreeing to land allotment. Many individual tribe members did not agree. They refused to have their names added to the tribal rolls. Allotment could not take place until the government knew who was qualified to receive land. As a result, the lands of the Five Civilized Tribes remained Indian Territory.

Twin Territories

In May 1890 Congress officially named the settled lands Oklahoma Territory. The boundary between Oklahoma Territory and Indian Territory ran diagonally from northeast to southwest. Guthrie became the capital of the Oklahoma Territory.

The two territories were called the Twin Territories. Now surrounded by states, people in the Twin Territories wanted statehood, too.

The Forty-Sixth State

Congress thought the Twin Territories should become one state—Oklahoma. The Five Civilized Tribes, however, wanted Indian Territory to be a separate state—the

State of Sequoyah. Congress rejected this idea and decided to merge the two territories into one state. Delegates from both territories were called to create a constitution. And on November 16, 1907, Congress ratified the constitution and Oklahoma became the forty-sixth state to join the Union.

When the Twin Territories became the state of Oklahoma, Indian Territory ceased to exist. Consequently, the government of each tribe was dissolved. Still, the Five Civilized Tribes continued to own the land as a tribe—for a while. They successfully delayed completing the allotment process seven years after statehood. On June 30, 1914, however, the allotment of Indian land in

Oklahoma City, the state's capital, was once a small homesteader settlement.

A cowboy looks back to make sure his herd of cattle is moving.

Oklahoma, including that of the Five Civilized Tribes, was completed.

Oklahoma Today

Today Oklahoma is home to thirty-nine tribes with headquarters in the state. Although all tribes suffered damage to their culture during resettlement, they are currently focused on preserving their cultures while sharing in the American dream. Their children attend public schools. Tribal elders, however, teach the young people to speak the native languages that were once forbidden and almost lost.

In almost one hundred years since gaining statehood, Oklahoma has been through economic boom and disas-

An oil refinery and high-rise buildings form the skyline of Tulsa, once the oil capital of the world.

Boomers and Sooners

ter. Oil was first discovered in 1859, and the first commercial well, the Nellie Johnstone 1, came in on April 15, 1897. An oil boom was in progress in 1907 when Oklahoma became a state. With the discovery of a rich oil field in northeastern Oklahoma, Tulsa became the oil capital of the world. After several decades, however, oil production slowed and the boom ended. Some people left Oklahoma during natural and economic disasters including the dust bowl and Great Depression. Many, however, stayed and thrived as cattle ranchers, farmers, truckers, teachers, bankers, and business executives.

Oklahoma is a mix of the old and new. While tall office buildings grace the skyline of Oklahoma City and Tulsa, Indians still dance to the beat of the drum, and cowboys ride and rope.

Facts About Oklahoma

State capital: Oklahoma City

Land area: 69,919 square miles

State nickname: The Sooner State

State song: "Oklahoma," composed and written by Richard Rodgers and Oscar Hammerstein

State tree: redbud

State bird: scissor-tailed flycatcher

State flower: mistletoe

Natural resources: fertile soil, granite, natural gas, lakes, petroleum, and grasslands for grazing cattle

Mountain ranges: Ouachita, Arbuckle, Wichita, and Kiamichi

Trees: mesquite, pecan, oak, cottonwood, pine, cedar, and poplar

Flowers: clover, Indian blanket, mistletoe, and sunflower

Animals: armadillo, buffalo, coyote, cottontail rabbit, jackrabbit, opossum, raccoon, skunk, squirrel, white-tailed deer, and wolf

Birds: blue jay, buzzard, cardinal, crow, finch, mocking-bird, owl, purple martin, raven, sparrow, swallow, and various hawks

Facts About Oklahoma

Important crops: alfalfa, cotton, maize, oats, peaches, pecans, peanuts, soybeans, sunflowers, watermelon, and wheat

Population (2000 census): 3,450,654

Persons per square mile (2000 census): 50.3 (U.S., 79.6)

Ethnic mix: white, 76.2%; Native American, 7.9%; African American, 7.6%; Hispanic or Latino, 5.2%; Asian, 1.4%; and Polynesian, 0.1% (Oklahoma has the largest Native American population of any state—7.9%. For comparison, the total U.S. Native American population is only 0.9%.)

Glossary

allotment: Land granted each qualified member of a tribe before a reservation was opened for white settlement.

artifact: A recently discovered object that was used in ancient times.

band: A group of Indians that unite under one leader. Some tribes are made up of several bands.

bishop: A high-ranking official in the Catholic Church.

dominate: To control.

encroach: To trespass or crowd into another's area.

entice: To persuade someone to do something.

Indian Country: Land left to the Indians west of the Mississippi.

Indian Territory: Indian Country reduced to the area that is now Oklahoma and Kansas, which was then shrunk to the area that is now southeastern Oklahoma.

legend: A story handed down through generations, believed to be based on history and possibly true, but usually is not.

pelts: Fur-bearing animal skins that have been tanned.

removal: The process of forcing a tribe to move from their homelands to Indian Territory.

tepee: Portable Indian homes made of skins stretched over long poles tied together at the top to form a pyramid.

tributaries: Streams, creeks, and small rivers that flow into a larger river.

For Further Exploration

Books

Nancy Antle, *Beautiful Land: A Story of the Oklahoma Land Rush*. New York: Viking Penguin, 1996. *Beautiful Land* tells the story of the April 22, 1889, land run.

William Durbin, *The Journal of C.J. Jackson, a Dust Bowl Migrant, Oklahoma to California, 1935*. New York: Scholastic Trade, 2002. This is the story of a thirteen-year-old boy living in the Oklahoma panhandle during one of the most difficult times in Oklahoma history—the dust bowl.

Bill Lund, *The Cherokee Indians*. Mankato, MN: Bridgestone Books, 1997. This book takes a look at the past and present lives of the Cherokee people.

Cynthia Leitich Smith, *Jingle Dancer*. New York: William Morrow, 2000. *Jingle Dancer* is the story of an Oklahoma Creek Nation girl learning about her heritage and culture as she prepares to perform in the jingle dance.

Joyce Carol Thomas, *I Have Heard of a Land*. New York: HarperCollins, 1999. This is the story of an African American woman who stakes a homestead in Oklahoma Territory.

Websites

The Folsom Culture (www.csasi.org). This page is filled with photos of spearheads including one found near Anadarko at the Blackwater site.

Oklahoma

Indian Territory (www.rootsweb.com). This Web page displays maps of Indian Country and Indian Territory from the early 1700s to 1889.

Famous Oklahomans (www.odoc.state.ok.us). This web page has a list of famous people from Oklahoma and tells what they do and where they were born.

Index

Oklahoma

Picture Credits

About the Author

Deanne Durrett is the author of nonfiction books for kids. Ms. Durrett is a native Oklahoman whose great-grandfather lived in Oklahoma before statehood and the land run of 1889. She now lives in a retirement resort community in Arizona with her husband, Dan. Other members of the household include Einstein (a mini-schnauzer) and Willie (an Abysinnian cat).